MATH SERIES

ADVANCED
SUBTRACTION

by S. Harold Collins

Book design by Kathy Kifer

Copyright © 1987 Stanley H. Collins

Published by:
Garlic Press
605 Powers St.
Eugene, OR 97402

ISBN 0-931993-16-4
Order Number GP-016

www.garlicpress.com

To Parents and Teachers,

The Advanced Straight Forward Math Series has been designed for parents and teachers of children. This is the subtraction book. It is a straightforward, sequenced presentation of advanced subtraction skills. It assumes that basic subtraction facts have already been learned (if not, consult our first series: **The Straight Forward Math Series**).

These steps are suggested for mastery of advanced subtraction skills:

- Give the **Basic Facts Review** (page 1) to assure competency in basic subtraction facts. The test has 100 problems and is arranged to group facts (see Answers, page 30, for a display of facts).

  If knowledge of Basic Facts is not demonstrated, do not go on to the next level. Master Basic Facts first, they are crucial to subtraction success in this advanced series.

- Give **Beginning Assessment Test** to determine where to start Practice Sheets. The Beginning Assessement Test (page 2) will tell which advanced subtraction skills are sound and which need attention. Begin Practice Sheets where the Beginning Assessment Test shows that subtraction errors start.

  Look at the Beginning Assessement Test. If you consult the Answers on page 30, you will see that the problems are arranged in groupings. Each grouping is a skill. Each skill is sequential and requires mastery before a higher skill level can be started.

- Start **Practice Sheets** at the appropriate skill level as determined from the Beginning Assessment Test. Do not skip levels once begun; build to mastery of all skills.

  Practice Sheets are given for each skill level to provide ample practice.

  Set a standard to move from one subtraction level to the next; either a percentage correct or a number correct.

- Give **Review Sheets** after completion of each section.

- Give **Section Diagnostic Test** as a final measure of a particular section. Section Diagnostic Tests are arranged to identify problems which may still exist with a particular skill (much like the Beginning Assessment Test).

  Set a standard to move from one section to the next. If that standard is not met, go back, focus on problem skills with Practice Sheets or similar materials.

- Give **Final Assessment Test** to measure all advanced subtraction skills. Compare the change from the Beginning Assessment Test.

Table of Contents

Basic Facts Review

16 - 9	10 - 8	9 - 7	8 - 4	6 - 3	6 - 2	4 - 1	0 - 0	5 - 0	8 - 0
14 - 6	11 - 9	9 - 8	11 - 7	9 - 4	7 - 3	8 - 2	5 - 1	1 - 0	6 - 0
5 - 5	15 - 6	12 - 9	17 - 8	12 - 7	10 - 4	8 - 3	7 - 2	6 - 1	2 - 0
15 - 7	6 - 5	14 - 6	13 - 9	16 - 8	13 - 7	11 - 4	9 - 3	9 - 2	7 - 1
18 - 8	13 - 7	7 - 5	13 - 6	14 - 9	15 - 8	14 - 7	12 - 4	11 - 3	10 - 2
4 - 4	14 - 8	14 - 7	8 - 5	12 - 6	15 - 9	14 - 8	15 - 7	13 - 4	12 - 3
13 - 3	5 - 4	15 - 8	15 - 7	9 - 5	11 - 6	16 - 9	13 - 8	16 - 7	14 - 4
2 - 2	4 - 3	6 - 4	16 - 8	16 - 7	14 - 5	10 - 6	17 - 9	12 - 8	17 - 7
13 -10	3 - 2	5 - 3	7 - 4	17 - 8	7 - 7	13 - 5	9 - 6	18 - 9	11 - 8
11 -10	17 -10	4 - 2	6 - 3	8 - 4	9 - 8	8 - 7	12 - 5	8 - 6	19 - 9

Beginning Assessment Test

77 - 3	89 - 6	68 - 22	29 - 9	36 - 14	97 - 43

24 - 5	42 - 8	80 - 36	51 - 8	56 - 18	72 - 68

883 - 30	747 - 24	882 - 631	165 - 56	276 - 38	493 - 27

674 - 146	813 - 459	435 - 247	644 - 176	657 - 268	916 - 548

800 - 564	910 - 351	407 - 239	500 - 155	820 - 276	704 - 306

4,276 - 357	7,842 - 1,986	56,235 - 24,891	84,531 - 65,974

2 digits − 1 digit

no regrouping

24 − 3	38 − 6	45 − 4	59 − 8	67 − 3	42 − 2	88 − 5
17 − 6	97 − 5	76 − 4	29 − 9	54 − 0	75 − 2	37 − 6
26 − 2	36 − 5	48 − 3	89 − 6	19 − 5	67 − 7	55 − 1
52 − 2	16 − 4	27 − 5	38 − 7	56 − 2	83 − 3	76 − 2
79 − 0	88 − 8	96 − 3	69 − 7	47 − 4	82 − 1	58 − 3
66 − 2	59 − 6	77 − 6	88 − 4	19 − 7	34 − 3	38 − 5
27 − 4	38 − 8	18 − 5	65 − 2	77 − 3	80 − 0	49 − 2

2 digits − 2 digits

no regrouping

23	15	77	49	33	58	62
- 22	- 11	- 34	- 27	- 12	- 24	- 50

30	49	34	66	31	55	24
- 20	- 14	- 11	- 25	- 21	- 40	- 12

42	19	66	43	37	68	75
- 22	- 15	- 12	- 20	- 16	- 24	- 42

29	81	35	78	56	47	38
- 18	- 50	- 14	- 35	- 33	- 14	- 15

57	46	63	58	74	87	84
- 23	- 14	- 31	- 32	- 23	- 22	- 34

88	95	23	90	89	39	54
- 14	- 63	- 12	- 70	- 52	- 31	- 40

87	67	64	93	76	82	74
- 55	- 10	- 61	- 62	- 55	- 22	- 12

2 digits — 2 digits

no regrouping

43 - 30	39 - 31	89 - 52	67 - 57	86 - 75	99 - 81	79 - 10
79 - 23	68 - 47	75 - 42	97 - 50	89 - 64	96 - 35	99 - 76
68 - 22	91 - 71	81 - 30	97 - 63	86 - 71	56 - 20	85 - 35
32 - 10	58 - 15	94 - 43	30 - 20	83 - 63	76 - 73	74 - 40
88 - 40	79 - 50	57 - 36	74 - 41	76 - 44	96 - 86	69 - 37
24 - 12	25 - 13	28 - 14	36 - 14	69 - 16	68 - 45	59 - 36
85 - 23	69 - 14	23 - 21	99 - 83	78 - 25	83 - 73	97 - 43

5

3 digits — 2 digits

no regrouping

```
  166        178        194        167        295        234        486
-  23      -  44      -  32      -  37      -  64      -  20      -  65


  378        388        299        485        189        558        550
-  52      -  55      -  46      -  12      -  24      -  51      -  30


  654        789        577        488        797        684        127
-  41      -  43      -  24      -  73      -  82      -  34      -  27


  586        946        879        558        456        786        999
-  24      -  32      -  78      -  27      -  20      -  71      -  76


  467        687        791        368        556        981        897
-  10      -  55      -  71      -  22      -  45      -  30      -  63


  288        679        374        457        789        385        795
-  48      -  50      -  41      -  36      -  62      -  45      -  33


  397        437        899        563        817        974        184
-  37      -  35      -  75      -  51      -  15      -  74      -  22
```

3 digits — 3 digits

no regrouping

436 - 324	337 - 104	675 - 175	588 - 314	874 - 123	682 - 222	476 - 355
137 - 126	672 - 300	948 - 623	258 - 242	490 - 320	869 - 617	172 - 120
878 - 546	678 - 237	587 - 380	979 - 665	869 - 402	807 - 401	569 - 304
467 - 312	198 - 137	810 - 300	598 - 334	277 - 213	579 - 243	400 - 400
388 - 140	876 - 254	929 - 517	965 - 754	259 - 136	879 - 306	979 - 854
349 - 127	475 - 243	678 - 345	357 - 154	846 - 213	998 - 426	567 - 243
792 - 371	987 - 823	699 - 323	436 - 324	789 - 779	837 - 525	777 - 234

3 digits - 3 digits

no regrouping

883 - 130	456 - 112	979 - 436	654 - 320	865 - 622	479 - 214	898 - 424
588 - 237	589 - 111	768 - 335	878 - 321	515 - 313	767 - 343	659 - 127
959 - 235	794 - 241	962 - 330	869 - 124	878 - 856	963 - 231	508 - 407
499 - 419	563 - 242	888 - 123	396 - 241	465 - 300	747 - 224	773 - 110
979 - 246	942 - 931	479 - 273	964 - 304	831 - 731	291 - 170	648 - 333
787 - 346	680 - 240	111 - 101	787 - 444	668 - 226	406 - 206	976 - 543
582 - 271	769 - 340	668 - 334	497 - 142	882 - 631	523 - 303	987 - 456

Review Sheet

no regrouping

38 - 6	77 - 34	67 - 3	33 - 12	88 - 5	62 - 50	34 - 3
99 - 79	17 - 6	19 - 15	69 - 7	37 - 16	88 - 8	75 - 42
789 - 78	95 - 63	77 - 6	58 - 32	385 - 45	84 - 34	48 - 3
89 - 52	90 - 70	93 - 62	563 - 51	78 - 35	89 - 52	46 - 14
588 - 314	66 - 22	476 - 355	78 - 35	807 - 405	981 - 30	876 - 254
627 - 24	678 - 345	189 - 24	846 - 213	55 - 40	567 - 243	159 - 136
989 - 823	899 - 75	436 - 324	999 - 645	789 - 779	789 - 62	777 - 234

Section
Diagnostic Test

no regrouping

96 - 3	18 - 5	77 - 3	80 - 0	47 - 4	58 - 4	99 - 7
88 - 40	57 - 36	76 - 44	96 - 86	59 - 36	28 - 14	99 - 83
78 - 25	69 - 16	94 - 43	97 - 63	56 - 20	75 - 42	79 - 23
39 - 31	89 - 6	86 - 75	485 - 12	96 - 35	56 - 6	684 - 34
679 - 50	374 - 41	789 - 62	184 - 22	974 - 43	899 - 75	437 - 35
456 - 112	865 - 622	898 - 424	589 - 111	515 - 313	659 - 127	959 - 235
499 - 419	648 - 333	582 - 271	497 - 142	882 - 631	406 - 206	987 - 456

2 digits — 1 digit

regrouping

24 - 5	30 - 5	42 - 8	30 - 4	62 - 8	32 - 7	51 - 6
74 - 6	22 - 9	42 - 6	86 - 8	92 - 3	20 - 3	63 - 8
46 - 7	51 - 2	94 - 8	74 - 9	51 - 8	63 - 6	31 - 9
30 - 1	53 - 5	66 - 9	73 - 7	80 - 5	65 - 9	95 - 7
61 - 3	78 - 9	70 - 7	52 - 5	67 - 8	74 - 5	81 - 7
32 - 6	45 - 8	36 - 9	43 - 5	31 - 4	62 - 5	46 - 8
54 - 8	35 - 7	72 - 8	31 - 3	64 - 7	33 - 9	22 - 8

2 digits − 1 digit

regrouping

60 − 6	32 − 4	57 − 8	44 − 6	83 − 8	76 − 7	61 − 5
41 − 7	63 − 7	75 − 9	24 − 5	90 − 7	84 − 8	53 − 7
73 − 4	65 − 8	81 − 6	40 − 5	36 − 9	52 − 7	74 − 9
62 − 8	54 − 7	71 − 2	23 − 5	46 − 7	96 − 8	21 − 9
68 − 9	50 − 4	92 − 6	21 − 5	47 − 9	35 − 8	72 − 8
24 − 9	57 − 9	98 − 9	33 − 9	70 − 9	44 − 7	56 − 8
50 − 3	72 − 8	88 − 9	33 − 7	47 − 9	31 − 3	42 − 9

2 digits − 2 digits

regrouping

51 − 32	42 − 18	31 − 25	57 − 29	60 − 53	41 − 24	52 − 37
93 − 66	74 − 58	80 − 36	92 − 13	81 − 43	70 − 47	92 − 26
85 − 19	23 − 17	86 − 78	75 − 28	91 − 36	62 − 15	73 − 54
80 − 48	97 − 78	88 − 29	90 − 55	21 − 17	71 − 38	64 − 49
62 − 24	94 − 78	64 − 35	56 − 18	81 − 59	44 − 26	72 − 43
95 − 46	51 − 27	68 − 19	40 − 12	72 − 68	85 − 18	61 − 32
42 − 16	45 − 19	50 − 21	84 − 67	73 − 44	92 − 45	74 − 15

2 digits − 2 digits

regrouping

90 − 24	51 − 15	98 − 49	60 − 56	52 − 27	92 − 39	61 − 43
85 − 26	65 − 47	93 − 66	50 − 19	72 − 15	81 − 59	36 − 28
77 − 49	67 − 28	96 − 27	83 − 44	51 − 34	91 − 28	40 − 37
86 − 29	63 − 15	84 − 59	72 − 35	60 − 27	95 − 28	82 − 36
80 − 15	73 − 29	64 − 38	33 − 17	90 − 14	92 − 28	81 − 17
84 − 66	51 − 27	44 − 17	93 − 65	40 − 18	77 − 29	92 − 66
64 − 27	88 − 59	92 − 13	64 − 17	95 − 78	50 − 17	92 − 45

Zero — Concept

regrouping

20 - 7	50 - 4	40 - 5	90 - 6	60 - 8	80 - 9
30 - 3	60 - 23	20 - 5	60 - 17	90 - 4	40 - 22
50 - 9	70 - 53	80 - 8	90 - 86	30 - 9	70 - 36
90 - 71	60 - 42	40 - 7	50 - 5	30 - 8	60 - 33
20 - 19	90 - 41	80 - 6	50 - 8	70 - 65	40 - 17
90 - 53	80 - 19	60 - 21	20 - 10	70 - 62	50 - 25
70 - 32	90 - 56	80 - 21	30 - 9	60 - 13	80 - 14

Review Sheet

regrouping: 2 digits – 1 digit, 2 digits – 2 digits, Zero Concept

42 − 8	51 − 6	74 − 6	86 − 8	63 − 8	46 − 7	94 − 9
30 − 4	66 − 9	73 − 7	20 − 3	74 − 5	31 − 4	40 − 7
62 −24	80 − 2	94 −78	70 − 5	56 −18	70 − 9	44 −26
82 −26	85 −18	20 −14	70 −47	56 −47	62 −17	93 −29
50 −23	44 − 7	72 −53	80 −29	86 −18	40 − 4	70 −24
88 −29	90 −54	71 −26	82 −79	73 −27	60 −17	85 −17
31 −25	41 −24	93 −66	85 −19	75 −28	91 −36	21 −17

Section
Diagnostic Test

regrouping: 2 digits – 1 digit, 2 digits – 2 digits, Zero Concept

42 - 8	51 - 32	60 - 56	98 - 9	22 - 8	73 - 44
86 - 8	57 - 29	40 - 18	65 - 47	81 - 7	68 - 19
51 - 8	86 - 78	90 - 24	33 - 7	63 - 6	84 - 67
73 - 7	44 - 26	20 - 9	96 - 27	52 - 5	21 - 17
78 - 9	72 - 68	70 - 23	44 - 7	66 - 9	75 - 28
35 - 7	46 - 19	80 - 42	64 - 38	74 - 5	91 - 36

3 digits — 2 digits

regrouping

| 365 | 573 | 944 | 180 | 165 | 420 | 276 |
| - 38 | - 54 | - 18 | - 27 | - 56 | - 12 | - 38 |

| 874 | 156 | 971 | 356 | 393 | 937 | 583 |
| - 59 | - 37 | - 65 | - 29 | - 17 | - 29 | - 26 |

| 690 | 452 | 976 | 643 | 862 | 474 | 587 |
| - 47 | - 46 | - 28 | - 18 | - 25 | - 37 | - 59 |

| 591 | 765 | 850 | 891 | 273 | 784 | 555 |
| - 53 | - 18 | - 26 | - 27 | - 39 | - 58 | - 17 |

| 878 | 562 | 493 | 961 | 875 | 962 | 391 |
| - 69 | - 24 | - 27 | - 33 | - 58 | - 29 | - 46 |

| 465 | 770 | 977 | 473 | 591 | 685 | 582 |
| - 26 | - 63 | - 29 | - 39 | - 62 | - 49 | - 58 |

| 990 | 372 | 394 | 772 | 234 | 157 | 982 |
| - 36 | - 67 | - 57 | - 24 | - 15 | - 49 | - 25 |

3 digits — 2 digits

regrouping

638 - 48	527 - 92	345 - 71	805 - 63	782 - 91	449 - 78	276 - 85
950 - 60	564 - 82	847 - 84	727 - 43	333 - 82	971 - 81	218 - 43
409 - 92	625 - 92	946 - 62	708 - 82	246 - 93	828 - 38	967 - 93
459 - 77	728 - 85	346 - 51	864 - 74	979 - 96	615 - 22	837 - 72
426 - 53	803 - 61	958 - 96	220 - 40	127 - 96	448 - 87	418 - 87
156 - 82	223 - 60	317 - 65	867 - 73	768 - 84	545 - 91	172 - 90
467 - 94	826 - 74	206 - 45	167 - 80	487 - 95	527 - 75	902 - 61

3 digits — 3 digits

regrouping

250 - 125	474 - 147	620 - 467	432 - 156	581 - 347	960 - 427
936 - 479	616 - 207	543 - 228	613 - 246	822 - 665	439 - 276
728 - 562	448 - 239	890 - 428	537 - 298	511 - 189	515 - 245
735 - 368	252 - 129	256 - 138	821 - 378	601 - 372	910 - 123
743 - 567	543 - 315	907 - 555	718 - 445	875 - 794	872 - 439
535 - 159	743 - 253	920 - 632	403 - 154	883 - 128	200 - 127
601 - 117	842 - 257	714 - 435	527 - 294	621 - 198	623 - 519

3 digits — 3 digits

regrouping

336 - 129	972 - 196	980 - 748	753 - 497	672 - 654	523 - 156
864 - 679	280 - 203	602 - 257	971 - 565	845 - 378	393 - 214
492 - 157	381 - 292	354 - 117	836 - 268	486 - 278	910 - 285
812 - 183	674 - 146	910 - 351	424 - 218	643 - 464	767 - 439
625 - 356	700 - 237	943 - 737	781 - 494	533 - 289	427 - 208
804 - 228	357 - 199	450 - 287	865 - 579	642 - 285	784 - 358
732 - 459	621 - 149	813 - 459	800 - 564	823 - 476	415 - 247

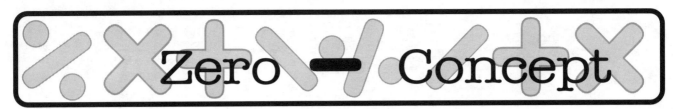

Zero − Concept

regrouping

420 - 115	807 - 174	870 - 326	906 - 285	750 - 748	609 - 362
310 - 168	904 - 365	720 - 439	807 - 259	630 - 573	505 - 278
605 - 164	303 - 257	809 - 233	906 - 148	200 - 184	608 - 399
600 - 247	502 - 208	900 - 183	801 - 556	400 - 292	703 - 187
410 - 215	500 - 333	620 - 227	700 - 234	906 - 207	800 - 76
200 - 189	908 - 219	800 - 274	506 - 158	600 - 447	701 - 528

Review Sheet

regrouping: 3 digits – 2 digits, 3 digits – 3 digits, Zero Concept

573 - 54	474 - 147	165 - 56	581 - 347	583 - 26	910 - 123
850 - 26	543 - 315	273 - 39	907 - 555	391 - 46	875 - 794
743 - 253	345 - 71	250 - 125	333 - 82	527 - 294	979 - 96
336 - 129	850 - 748	427 - 208	900 - 183	943 - 737	703 - 187
410 - 215	980 - 748	500 - 333	845 - 378	906 - 207	424 - 218
956 - 98	451 - 287	220 - 41	813 - 459	127 - 38	865 - 579
582 - 193	800 - 274	712 - 387	701 - 528	923 - 468	808 - 219

Section
Diagnostic Test

regrouping: 3 digits – 2 digits, 3 digits – 3 digits, Zero Concept

623 - 519	883 - 128	772 - 439	256 - 138	652 - 129	543 - 228
868 - 372	939 - 266	647 - 457	714 - 244	658 - 283	527 - 453
753 - 497	381 - 292	325 - 157	767 - 439	828 - 359	533 - 289
870 - 326	607 - 162	700 - 234	906 - 148	600 - 347	750 - 743
672 - 654	971 - 565	393 - 214	792 - 357	486 - 248	564 - 328
428 - 264	955 - 273	827 - 384	617 - 175	838 - 567	667 - 482
911 - 428	462 - 377	964 - 488	864 - 579	822 - 183	643 - 464

4 digits − 3 digits

regrouping

4,483 - 567	4,960 - 793	9,838 - 873	5,513 - 426	6,076 - 286
7,672 - 269	8,362 - 388	3,845 - 375	2,712 - 796	1,864 - 679
6,812 - 946	5,784 - 895	3,017 - 236	4,584 - 663	2,172 - 263
9,354 - 265	8,765 - 924	6,572 - 686	1,472 - 463	3,876 - 795
7,842 - 658	5,270 - 952	2,700 - 943	6,764 - 377	8,101 - 654
3,336 - 274	1,278 - 589	7,054 - 768	4,972 - 995	2,312 - 887

4 digits − 4 digits

regrouping

4,894 − 2,983	5,867 − 4,948	6,002 − 2,453	5,554 − 2,564	4,348 − 3,835
6,754 − 4,675	8,943 − 2,857	7,127 − 3,508	4,895 − 1,627	7,046 − 2,648
5,891 − 4,682	9,476 − 4,897	8,508 − 4,962	6,600 − 5,755	7,342 − 1,565
4,384 − 2,967	3,576 − 2,287	5,867 − 2,987	8,572 − 4,963	1,272 − 1,178
5,726 − 3,958	6,875 − 3,497	9,947 − 9,856	4,070 − 2,488	7,274 − 5,368
9,435 − 2,786	7,098 − 4,289	1,876 − 1,097	8,471 − 1,683	6,872 − 5,947

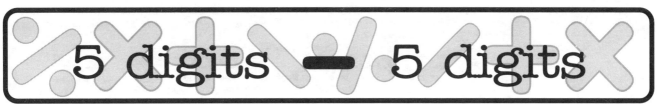

regrouping

32,005 - 11,564	48,236 - 21,892	65,408 - 22,986	78,243 - 29,354	98,642 - 27,651
42,726 - 23,815	63,594 - 14,672	56,482 - 29,278	40,000 - 26,326	97,245 - 96,176
33,821 - 15,678	20,476 - 17,368	15,167 - 12,368	97,624 - 64,837	47,620 - 18,547
21,246 - 10,745	36,896 - 25,897	74,286 - 22,194	86,723 - 47,268	60,727 - 41,837
60,002 - 42,673	48,274 - 23,186	75,183 - 28,426	40,780 - 16,942	86,271 - 79,452

Review Sheet

regrouping: 4 digits – 3 digits, 4 digits – 4 digits, 5 digits – 5 digits

8,309 - 457	9,456 - 8,697	1,001 - 927	4,583 - 1,723	2,312 - 887
9,806 - 2,947	4,972 - 985	8,548 - 6,669	7,054 - 658	3,865 - 1,974
7,842 - 658	2,896 - 1,994	1,267 - 258	9,341 - 3,295	7,062 - 975
5,906 - 2,457	6,749 - 878	6,223 - 2,636	1,127 - 848	9,947 - 9,858
47,236 - 21,892	100,000 - 73,498		56,427 - 29,836	12,072 - 10,568
68,875 - 32,086	77,844 - 24,477		82,009 - 35,467	92,827 - 39,635

Final Assessment Test

89 - 52	167 - 37	882 - 631	795 - 33	987 - 456	768 - 336
98 - 49	51 - 34	92 - 28	82 - 56	75 - 28	73 - 26
765 - 18	977 - 29	372 - 67	748 - 567	936 - 284	814 - 373
357 - 199	621 - 149	971 - 565	872 - 186	523 - 147	743 - 265
700 - 524	801 - 137	670 - 485	900 - 462	509 - 269	403 - 148

64,005 - 21,564	9,786 - 8,898	27,142 - 16,193	87,942 - 28,853

ANSWERS

The **Basic Facts Review** has facts arranged diagonally.
This diagonal arrangement quickly identifies facts
which are firm and facts which need attention.

Basic Facts Review, page 1.

16−9=7	10−8=2	9−7=2	8−4=4	6−3=3	6−2=4	4−1=3	0−0=0	5−0=5	8−0=8	0
14−6=8	11−9=2	9−8=1	11−7=4	9−4=5	7−3=4	8−2=6	5−1=4	1−0=1	6−0=6	0
5−5=0	15−6=9	12−9=3	17−8=9	12−7=5	10−4=6	8−3=5	7−2=5	6−1=5	2−0=2	0
15−7=8	6−5=1	14−6=8	13−9=4	16−8=8	13−7=6	11−4=7	9−3=6	9−2=7	7−1=6	1
18−8=10	13−7=6	7−5=2	13−6=7	14−9=5	15−8=7	14−7=7	12−4=8	11−3=8	10−2=8	2
4−4=0	14−8=6	14−7=7	8−5=3	12−6=6	15−9=6	14−8=6	15−7=8	13−4=9	12−3=9	3
13−3=10	5−4=1	15−8=7	15−7=8	9−5=4	11−6=5	16−9=7	13−8=5	16−7=9	14−4=10	4
2−2=0	4−3=1	6−4=2	16−8=8	16−7=9	14−5=9	10−6=4	17−9=8	12−8=4	17−7=10	7
13−10=3	3−2=1	5−3=2	7−4=3	17−8=9	7−7=0	13−5=8	9−6=3	18−9=9	11−8=3	8
11−10=1	17−10=7	4−2=2	6−3=3	8−4=4	9−8=1	8−7=1	12−5=7	8−6=2	19−9=10	9
10	10	2	3	4	8	7	5	6		

Begin *Practice Sheets* at the skill level
where several errors occur.

Practice Sheet, page 3.

21	32	41	51	64	40	83
11	92	72	20	54	73	31
24	31	45	83	14	60	54
50	12	22	31	54	80	74
79	80	93	62	43	81	55
64	53	71	84	12	31	33
23	30	13	63	74	80	47

Practice Sheet, page 4.

1	4	43	22	21	34	12
10	35	23	41	10	15	12
20	4	54	23	21	44	33
11	31	21	43	23	33	23
34	32	32	26	51	65	50
74	32	11	20	37	8	14
32	57	3	31	21	60	62

Practice Sheet, page 5.

13	8	37	10	11	18	69
56	21	33	47	25	61	23
46	20	51	34	15	36	50
22	43	51	10	20	3	34
48	29	21	33	32	10	32
12	12	14	22	53	23	23
62	55	2	16	53	10	54

Beginning Assessment Test, page 2.

						Skill
77−3=74	89−6=83	68−22=46	29−9=20	36−14=22	97−43=54	2 digits − 1 digit / 2 digits − 2 digits no renaming
24−5=19	42−8=34	80−36=44	51−8=43	56−18=38	72−68=4	2 digits − 1 digit / 2 digits − 2 digits renaming
883−30=853	747−24=723	882−631=251	165−56=109	276−38=238	493−27=466	3 digits − 2 digits no renaming / 3 digits − 2 digits renaming
674−146=528	813−459=354	435−247=188	644−176=468	657−268=389	916−548=368	3 digits − 3 digits renaming
800−564=236	910−351=559	407−239=168	500−155=345	820−276=544	704−306=398	zero concept renaming
4276−357=3919	7842−1986=5856	56,235−24,891=31,344	84,531−65,974=18,557			multiple digits renaming

The **Beginning Assessment Test** is arranged horizontally
by skills. This arrangement will identify skills which are
firm and skills which need attention.

ANSWERS

Practice Sheet, page 6.

143	134	162	130	231	214	421
326	333	253	473	165	507	520
613	746	553	415	715	650	100
562	914	801	531	436	715	923
457	632	720	346	511	951	834
240	629	333	421	727	340	762
360	402	824	512	802	900	162

Practice Sheet, page 7.

112	233	500	274	751	460	121
11	372	325	16	170	252	52
332	441	207	314	467	406	265
155	61	510	264	64	336	0
248	622	412	211	123	573	125
222	232	333	203	633	572	324
421	164	376	112	10	312	543

Practice Sheet, page 8.

753	344	543	334	243	265	474
351	478	433	557	202	424	532
724	553	632	745	22	732	101
80	321	765	155	165	523	663
733	11	206	660	100	121	315
441	440	10	343	442	200	433
311	429	334	355	251	220	531

Review Sheet, page 9

32	43	64	21	83	12	31
20	11	4	62	21	80	33
711	32	71	26	340	50	45
37	20	31	512	43	37	32
274	44	121	43	402	951	622
603	333	165	633	15	324	23
166	824	112	354	10	727	543

Section Diagnostic Test, page 10.

The **Section Diagnostic Tests** are specially arranged, too. The arrangement helps to identify if there are still problems and for which skills those problems occur.

96 -3 **93**	18 -5 **13**	77 -3 **74**	80 -0 **80**	47 -4 **43**	58 -4 **54**	99 -7 **92**	2 digits - 1 digit no renaming
88 -40 **48**	57 -36 **21**	76 -44 **32**	96 -86 **10**	59 -36 **23**	28 -14 **14**	99 -83 **16**	2 digits - 2 digits no renaming
78 -25 **53**	69 -16 **53**	94 -43 **51**	97 -63 **34**	56 -20 **36**	75 -42 **33**	79 -23 **56**	2 digits - 2 digits no renaming
39 -31 **8**	89 -6 **83**	86 -75 **11**	485 -12 **473**	96 -35 **61**	56 -6 **50**	684 -34 **650**	mixed no renaming
679 -50 **629**	374 -41 **333**	789 -62 **727**	184 -22 **162**	974 -43 **931**	899 -75 **824**	437 -35 **402**	3 digits - 2 digits no renaming
456 -112 **344**	865 -622 **243**	898 -424 **474**	589 -111 **478**	515 -313 **202**	659 -127 **532**	959 -235 **724**	3 digits - 3 digits no renaming
499 -419 **80**	648 -333 **315**	582 -271 **311**	497 -142 **355**	882 -631 **251**	406 -206 **200**	987 -456 **531**	3 digits - 3 digits no renaming

ANSWERS

Practice Sheet, page 11.

19	25	34	26	54	25	45
68	13	36	78	89	17	55
39	49	86	65	43	57	22
29	48	57	66	75	56	88
58	69	63	47	59	69	74
26	37	27	38	27	57	38
46	28	64	28	57	24	14

Practice Sheet, page 12.

54	28	49	38	75	69	56
34	56	66	19	83	76	46
69	57	75	35	27	45	65
54	47	69	18	39	88	12
59	46	86	16	38	27	64
15	48	89	24	61	37	48
47	64	79	26	38	28	33

Practice Sheet, page 13.

19	24	6	28	7	17	15
27	16	44	79	38	23	66
66	6	8	47	55	47	19
32	19	59	35	4	33	15
38	16	29	38	22	18	29
49	24	49	28	4	67	29
26	26	29	17	29	47	59

Practice Sheet, page 14.

66	36	49	4	25	53	18
59	18	27	31	57	22	8
28	39	69	39	17	63	3
57	48	25	37	33	67	46
65	44	26	16	76	64	64
18	24	27	28	22	48	26
37	29	79	47	17	33	47

Practice Sheet, page 15.

13	46	35	84	52	71
27	37	15	43	86	18
41	17	72	4	21	34
19	18	33	45	22	27
1	49	74	42	5	23
37	61	39	10	8	25
38	34	59	21	47	66

Review Sheet, page 16.

34	45	68	78	55	39	85
26	57	66	17	69	27	33
38	78	16	65	38	61	18
56	67	6	23	9	45	64
27	37	19	51	68	36	46
59	36	45	3	46	43	68
6	17	27	66	47	55	4

ANSWERS

2 digits - 2 digits | 2 digits - 1 digit / 2 digits - 2 digits | 2 digits - 2 digits

42 − 8 = **34**	51 − 32 = **19**	60 − 56 = **4**	98 − 9 = **89**	22 − 8 = **14**	73 − 44 = **29**
86 − 8 = **78**	57 − 29 = **28**	40 − 18 = **22**	65 − 47 = **18**	81 − 7 = **74**	68 − 19 = **49**
51 − 8 = **43**	86 − 78 = **8**	90 − 24 = **66**	33 − 7 = **26**	63 − 6 = **57**	84 − 67 = **17**
73 − 7 = **66**	44 − 26 = **18**	20 − 9 = **11**	96 − 27 = **69**	52 − 5 = **47**	21 − 17 = **4**
78 − 9 = **69**	72 − 68 = **4**	70 − 23 = **47**	44 − 7 = **37**	66 − 9 = **57**	75 − 28 = **47**
35 − 7 = **28**	46 − 19 = **27**	80 − 42 = **38**	64 − 38 = **26**	74 − 5 = **69**	91 − 36 = **55**

digits - 1 digit   zero concept   2 digits - 1 digit

Practice Sheet, page 18.

327	519	926	153	109	408	238
815	119	906	327	376	908	557
643	406	948	625	837	437	528
538	747	824	864	234	726	538
809	538	466	928	817	933	345
439	707	948	434	529	636	524
954	305	337	748	219	108	957

Practice Sheet, 19.

590	435	274	742	691	371	191
890	482	763	684	251	890	175
317	533	884	626	153	790	874
382	643	295	790	883	593	765
373	742	862	180	31	361	331
74	163	252	794	684	454	82
373	752	161	87	392	452	841

Practice Sheet, page 20.

125	327	153	276	234	533
457	409	315	367	157	163
166	209	462	239	322	270
367	123	118	443	229	787
176	228	352	273	81	433
376	490	288	249	755	73
484	585	279	233	423	104

Practice Sheet, page 21.

207	776	232	256	18	367
185	77	345	406	467	179
335	89	237	568	208	625
629	528	559	206	179	328
269	463	206	287	244	219
576	158	163	286	357	426
273	472	354	236	347	168

Practice Sheet, page 22.

305	633	544	621	2	247
142	539	281	548	57	227
441	46	576	758	16	209
353	294	717	245	108	516
195	167	393	466	699	724
11	689	526	348	153	173

Practice Sheet, page 23.

519	327	109	234	557	787
824	228	234	352	345	81
490	274	125	251	233	883
207	102	219	717	206	516
195	232	167	467	699	206
858	164	179	354	89	286
389	526	325	173	455	589

ANSWERS

Section Diagnostic Test, page 24.

623 − 519 **104**	883 − 128 **755**	772 − 439 **333**	256 − 138 **118**	652 − 129 **523**	543 − 228 **315**	renaming 10's
868 − 372 **496**	939 − 266 **673**	647 − 457 **190**	714 − 244 **470**	658 − 283 **375**	527 − 453 **74**	renaming 100's
753 − 497 **256**	381 − 292 **89**	325 − 157 **168**	767 − 439 **328**	828 − 359 **469**	533 − 289 **244**	mixed renaming
870 − 326 **544**	607 − 162 **445**	700 − 234 **466**	906 − 148 **758**	600 − 347 **253**	750 − 743 **7**	zero concept
672 − 654 **18**	971 − 565 **406**	393 − 214 **179**	792 − 357 **435**	486 − 248 **238**	564 − 328 **236**	renaming 10's
428 − 264 **164**	955 − 273 **682**	827 − 384 **443**	617 − 175 **442**	838 − 567 **271**	667 − 482 **185**	renaming 100's
911 − 428 **483**	462 − 377 **85**	964 − 488 **476**	864 − 579 **285**	822 − 183 **639**	643 − 464 **179**	mixed renaming

Practice Sheet, page 25.

3916	4167	8965	5087	5790
7403	7974	3470	1916	1185
5866	4889	2781	3921	1909
9089	7841	5886	1009	3081
7184	4318	1757	6387	7447
3062	689	6286	3977	1425

Practice Sheet, page 26.

1911	919	3549	2990	513
2079	6086	3619	3268	4398
1209	4579	3546	845	5777
1417	1289	2880	3609	94
1768	3378	91	1582	1906
6649	2809	779	6788	925

Practice Sheet, page 27.

20,441	26,344	42,422	48,889	70,991
18,911	48,922	27,204	13,674	1069
18,143	3108	2799	32,787	29,073
10,501	10,999	52,092	39,455	18,890
17,329	25,088	46,757	23,838	6819

Practice Sheet, page 28.

7852	759	74	2860	1425
6859	3987	1879	6396	1891
7184	902	1009	6046	6087
3449	5871	3587	279	89
25,344	26,502	26,591	1504	
36,789	53,367	46,542	53,192	

The **Final Assessment Test** is arranged horizontally, by skills.

Final Assessment Test, page 29.

89 − 52 **37**	167 − 37 **130**	882 − 631 **251**	795 − 33 **762**	987 − 456 **531**	768 − 336 **432**	2 digits - 2 dig 3 digits - 2 dig 3 digits - 3 dig no renaming
98 − 49 **49**	51 − 34 **17**	92 − 28 **64**	82 − 56 **26**	75 − 28 **47**	73 − 26 **47**	2 digits - 2 dig renaming
765 − 18 **747**	977 − 29 **948**	372 − 67 **305**	748 − 567 **181**	936 − 284 **652**	814 − 373 **441**	3 digits - 2 dig 3 digits - 3 dig renaming
357 − 199 **158**	621 − 149 **472**	971 − 565 **406**	872 − 188 **686**	523 − 147 **376**	743 − 265 **478**	3 digits - 3 dig renaming
700 − 524 **176**	801 − 137 **664**	670 − 485 **185**	900 − 462 **438**	509 − 269 **240**	403 − 148 **255**	zero concept renaming
64,005 − 21,564 **42,441**		9786 − 8898 **888**		27,142 − 16,193 **10,949**	87,942 − 28,853 **59,089**	multiple digit renaming

34